THE OFFICIAL
CELTIC
ANNUAL
2003

Written by
Douglas Russell

A Grange Publication

© 2002. Published by Grange Communications Ltd., Edinburgh, under licence from Celtic Football Club. Printed in the EU.

ISBN 1-902704-28-2

£5.99

CONTENTS

HEADLINE NEWS

Celtic made the following football headlines during Season 2001/02. What was the occasion? The clue is in the date!

'Lambo to slaughter' Sunday Mail, 29.7.01

'Arena of dreams for brilliant Celts' Daily Mail, 9.8.01

'Knockout blows' Sunday Times, 16.9.01

'Celtic cheated out of fair share' Daily Mail, 19.9.01

'Moravcik sorcery steals the show on a night of magic' Daily Mail, 1.11.01

'Celtic make it 10 in a row' Sunday Times, 18.11.01

'It's all over' Daily Mail, 26.11.01

'Light years ahead' Sunday Herald, 16.12.01

'United green with envy' Sunday Herald, 30.12.01

'This one's for the Bhoys' Daily Mail, 31.1.02

ANSWERS ON PAGE 62

ANOTHER SEASON
IN THE SUN

A look back at the joys of Season 2001/02 and how Martin O'Neill's side retained their premiership crown (smashing the 100 point barrier in the process) with an almost faultless display of football at its best.

JULY 2001

To the rapturous acclaim of over 58,000 fans, club chairman Brian Quinn and manager Martin O'Neill unfurled the SPL 2000/01 Championship Flag at Celtic Park prior to the new season's opening league encounter at the end of July. Although visitors St. Johnstone threatened early on (mainly through their exciting Ivory Coast player Momo Sylla), it was 'Bhoy' defender Johan Mjallby who opened the actual scoring with a powerful header from Bobby Petta's cross in 38 minutes. After that, it was plain sailing and a somewhat rare second-half double from captain Paul Lambert (quite simply 'Man of the Match') ensured a comfortable start to the campaign and defence of their crown (3-0, 28.7.01). Prior to kick-off, striker supreme Henrik Larsson was presented with a commemorative silver shield to acknowledge his amazing tally of 53 goals from the previous year's campaigns. Although he did not score in today's game, there would be time enough for that!

AUGUST 2001

Four days later, Martin O'Neill took his side to Old Trafford (and a 67,000 sell-out crowd) for Ryan Giggs' testimonial match and returned later that night to Glasgow having witnessed Celtic notch their fourth straight win against Manchester United at this venue. The superb 4-3 victory was achieved with goals from Chris Sutton, Neil Lennon, Paul Lambert and Lubo Moravcik whilst the £42 million double act of Van Nistelrooy (2) and Veron netted for the home side. Earlier in the day, it was confirmed that John Hartson (from Coventry), Steve Guppy (from Leicester) and Momo Sylla (from St. Johnstone) were about to become Celts in transfer deals that would cost the club approximately £8 million in total.

5

Rugby Park, Kilmarnock (and a 5.35pm kick-off for the benefit of Sky TV subscribers) was the venue for the first domestic away game of the season. Despite a battling performance from the Ayrshire outfit, Henrik Larsson's goal (after scampering away from the blue and white rearguard in 74 minutes) ensured the safety of another three points (1-0, 4.8.01). Incidentally, this was the Swede's eighth strike in the last three meetings between the teams. New signing John Hartson appeared as a substitute early on (when Bobby Petta was injured) and turned in a fine, aggressive display but special praise went to Chris Sutton who was truly immense for all of the ninety minutes.

The following mid-week, in the first leg of the second preliminary round of the Champions League tournament, Celtic travelled to Holland to face a youthful Ajax side and recorded a magnificent 3-1 victory. First-half goals in the Amsterdam Arena from Bobby Petta and Didier Agathe were complimented by Chris Sutton's tremendous headed strike in the second period thus making the return leg in Glasgow, in two weeks time, surely more of a formality. After the game, Ajax coach Co Adriaanse agreed that his young side had been given a lesson in football.

Back on SPL duty, Hearts were hopeful visitors to the east end of the city on August 11. But, as on so many previous occasions, the capital outfit returned to Edinburgh empty handed with nothing to show for their efforts but a 2-0 defeat this time. A goal in each half from Henrik Larsson (the first was an 18 yard free-kick and the second, a delightful left-foot shot over the advancing Antti Niemi) secured victory. Another pleasing aspect of the afternoon was Chris Sutton's impressive display at the heart of Celtic's three-man defence. The player had previously filled this position to great acclaim in his days with Chelsea.

The first points of the campaign were dropped one week later when newly promoted Livingston held the league leaders to a 0-0 draw in West Lothian. A Larsson penalty save by goalkeeper Javier Sanchez Broto ensured a share of the spoils for Jim Leishman's Almondvale outfit who, incidentally, had also drawn with the other half of the Old Firm in Glasgow in the second game of the season. Back on European duty (August 22 and the return leg of the second preliminary round of the Champions League), the Scottish champions were beaten 1-0 at Celtic Park by visitors Ajax. In truth, the Dutch were by far the better team on the night and, but for goalkeeper Robert Douglas, could have won by a far greater margin. Nevertheless, an aggregate score of 3-2 saw the 'Bhoys' through to Champions League Group E where Juventus (Italy), Porto (Portugal) and Rosenborg (Norway) all lay in wait. On the day of the actual group stage draw in Monte Carlo, Henrik Larsson was also in town to receive the Golden Boot award in recognition of his achievement as Europe's top scorer for Season 2000/01.

The final game of the month was another trip to the east of the country but this time to Edinburgh, with Easter Road the venue and Hibernian the opponents. In a performance to relish, Celtic were really quite mesmerising and actually led 4-0 at the break after first-half goals from Lubo Moravcik (a stunning 25 yard strike in 16 mins), Chris Sutton (17 and 20 mins) and Henrik Larsson (30 mins). It was as good a first period as the fans had seen in a long, long time and the three valuable points (4-1, 25.8.01) protected their team's top of the table position after five domestic championship games played.

SEPTEMBER 2001

For the first time in the club's long history, when Dunfermline came calling on September 8, the starting line-up (minus those two usual suspects Robert Douglas and Paul Lambert) did not include a single Scottish born player. Nevertheless, two goals from a Slovak (Lubo Moravcik) and one from an Englishman (Chris Sutton) secured another impressive 'Hoops' victory (3-1, 8.9.01). This SPL fixture was also the game that introduced one Dianbobo Balde who, virtually overnight, became the cult figure known simply as Bobo to the Celtic park legions. Watching in the stands that afternoon was Rosenborg's assistant manager Ola By Rise as the Norwegians were due in Glasgow the following Wednesday on European duty. This game would end up being rescheduled due to the tragic events of September 11 in America.

A potentially hazardous trip to face Ivano Bonetti's Dundee in the City of Discovery resulted in an excellent 4-0 win, with second period goals from Henrik, Stilian Petrov and youngster Shaun Maloney complimenting the Swede's headed strike on the verge of half-time which had started the eventual rout. As the jubilant Celtic fans headed south back to Glasgow after this mid September trip, their thoughts were turning to pastures new and a rather different proposition – Turin and Juventus in the Champions League three days later. The game certainly appeared all over after Juve's French striker David Trezeguet had given the Serie A outfit a two goal cushion early in the second-half but the 'Bhoys' came roaring back like lions with a double of their own, courtesy of Petrov's shot and Larsson's penalty. At this stage, there seemed only one winner as Celts went for the kill but the Scottish champions were cruelly denied right at the end when Amoroso 'won' (and converted) a rather dubious penalty with just four minutes left on the clock (3-2, 18.9.01).

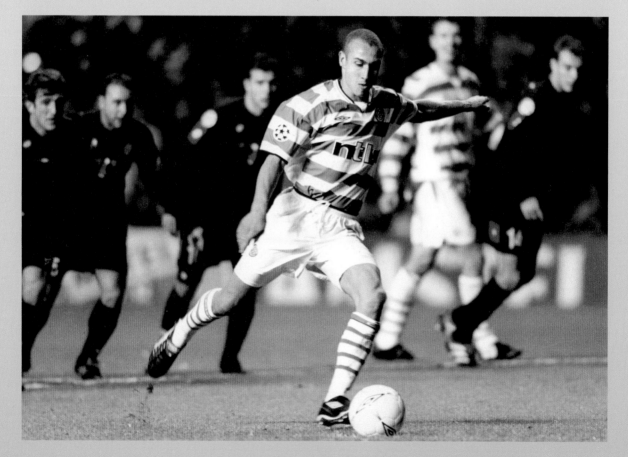

On home soil, it was now the turn of Aberdeen to offer some sort of spirited resistance but manager Ebbe Skovdahl (game 100 in charge of the granite city team) duly returned north having suffered his fourteenth consecutive Celtic park defeat as Pittodrie boss. Second-half goals from Larsson (the only Celt to start all games so far this campaign) and Petrov (now captain of his country Bulgaria) did the damage (2-0, 22.9.01). Skovdahl's side had now lost an astonishing 45 goals to Celtic in just three seasons! Back on midweek European business, Celtic achieved her maiden Champions League victory following an exciting duel with the mightily impressive Porto in Glasgow. Larsson's finish, from close in, was all that finally separated the teams (1-0, 25.9.01).

The month ended on another high with three valuable points gathered from the first Old Firm meeting, sending super Celts seven clear of their closest rivals in the race for the SPL title. For manager Martin O'Neill, the 2-0 triumph ensured Celtic's first back-to-back Ibrox victory in some 17 years and also 'his' third clean sheet in a row against Rangers. Although the home side actually dominated much of the play, goals from Petrov (a first-half free-kick) and Alan Thompson (a delightful curling right-foot shot at the end) were all that really mattered at the end of the day as the green machine relentlessly marched on.

OCTOBER 2001

Midfielder Thompson remained in the sport headlines as he was then the match winner himself when Rosenborg were beaten 1-0 in the rescheduled European game at Celtic Park on October 10. This result ensured maximum home points in the competition so far. Less than 72 hours later, Fir Park was the venue for an extremely close encounter with Motherwell. The match seemed to be heading for a 1-1 draw before Henke netted from the penalty spot right at the death (2-1, 13.10.01). For the record, Lubo Moravcik's sublime opener that day was his fourth goal in only five starts. In rather warmer climatic circumstances, a first minute goal by the Brazilian Clayton stunned our heroes in Portugal as Porto turned up the Champions League heat and proved far too strong on the night, eventually winning 3-0 with something to spare.

Bouncing back with a vengeance on the domestic trail, the 'Bhoys' hammered SPL visitors Dundee United 5-1 later that week in Glasgow. Both John Hartson (with a hat-trick) and Bobo Balde netted their first goals for the club whilst youngster Shaun Maloney claimed his second of the season. With the games now coming thick and fast, a trip to Trondheim in Norway was next on the European agenda. However, a certain Harald Brattbakk (whose historic goal against St. Johnstone had sealed the Scottish Championship for Celtic back in May 1998 and denied ten-in-a-row for arch rivals Rangers) was this time instrumental in his old team's downfall as Rosenborg secured a crucial 2-0 triumph. Indeed, the tall striker claimed both goals as well as winning a penalty for his team on the night. Back home, it was a case of the late, late show when Kilmarnock lost 1-0 at Celtic Park following Joos Valgaeren's injury time tap-in with 92 minutes on the clock. Better late than never!

Seven goal thrillers are a pretty rare occurrence these days but Celtic and Juventus managed to recreate the formula on the last day of the month. Although the aristocratic

Italians (who had already qualified for the next stage of the Champions League tournament) took the lead, goals from Valgaeren, Sutton (2) and Larsson meant a famous 4-3 victory on a night to remember for 57,717 fans in the east end of the city. It is worth remembering that Arsenal, Manchester United and Leeds had all failed to beat Juventus previously in year 2001. Special mention must go to Lubo Moravcik who was really quite sensational and controlled the game before being substituted late on. Unfortunately, with Porto winning 1-0 at home to Rosenborg (and it was close!), the 'Hoops' were denied third place in the group and would now play in the UEFA Cup.

NOVEMBER 2001

At the start of the month (on November 3 to be precise), it seemed for a time as if St. Johnstone, despite languishing at the foot of the table, might take a valuable point before Larsson's tremendous free-kick claimed all three right at the end of the McDiarmid Park encounter (2-1, 3.1.01). Shaun Maloney's four goal scoring spree was one of the evening's highlights when a total of eight were drilled past Stirling Albion in Round 3 of the CIS Insurance sponsored League Cup before a difficult trip to the Gorgie district of Edinburgh and top flight opponents Hearts on a very cold Saturday afternoon. Sadly, the subsequent 1-0 triumph (penalty-Larsson-goal) came at a high price as Didier Agathe was badly injured by a clumsy 'Jambo' tackle and would remain out of action until early February. Celtic, by the way, had just created a new club record of 10 consecutive wins in the SPL.

Robert Douglas was the undoubted hero when the 'Bhoys' travelled to Spain to face Valencia (beaten Champions League finalists for the last two years) in the first leg of their UEFA Cup third-round tie. The big 'keeper had pulled off a series of outstanding stops before Rodriguez netted some fifteen minutes in advance of the final whistle, giving his side the narrowest of winning margins (1-0, 22.11.01). After the game, his opposite number in the Valencia goal (Santiago Canizares) admitted that Douglas had made 'five or six saves of extraordinary quality.' Praise indeed from one of the best and someone at the top of his profession.

Viewed by a crowd of 59,609, the second Old Firm encounter of the season was, just like the first, an extremely close contest but once again Celts netted twice and were victorious (2-1, 25.11.01). Goals from Valgaeren and Larsson (a penalty) ensured the safety of another three points, lifting their side ten clear at the top after a fifth consecutive derby success in calendar year 2001. In the eyes of many neutrals, the league was now effectively over – even though Christmas celebrations were still some way off.

DECEMBER 2001

With another sound game in defence, Chris Sutton again displayed his versatility when Hibernian lost 3-0 in Glasgow. Neil Lennon's first of the season followed a double from John Hartson thus ensuring that the capital outfit returned home without a win at Celtic Park since 1992. A gulf of ten points now separated the top two after Rangers were held to a no scoring draw at Dens Park. Unfortunately European involvement for the meantime came to an end the following Thursday when, despite Celtic winning the actual game 1-0 to level the aggregate score, Valencia progressed to the next round of the UEFA Cup after a 5-4 penalty shoot-out triumph. Incidentally, Larsson's goal that night was number 17 in Europe for the Swede and set a new Celtic record, breaking that previously held by the legendary winger Jimmy Johnstone. Back on league duty in Fife, Dunfermline proved no match and were soundly beaten 4-0 on their own patch with John Hartson again claiming a double.

The Welshman then made it five goals in just three SPL encounters when Dundee came calling on December 15. Ivano Bonetti's cosmopolitan side had actually led at the interval but second-half goals from Larsson, Sutton and the aforementioned Hartson kept the 'Hoops' on course with consecutive league win number fourteen (3-1,15.12.01). With Larsson, Lennon, Lambert and Thompson all rested, Celtic still proved too strong for Livingston and progressed to the semi-final stage of the CIS sponsored League Cup. Headed goals by Balde and then Hartson (five minutes from the end) meant a Hampden date with Rangers in early February.

Then an almost surreal thing happened – the champions were defeated in an SPL match! Victors Aberdeen, who had only managed to beat the 'Bhoys' once in their previous 25 meetings, won 2-0 on a cold, snowy Pittodrie night, giving the home support an unexpected pre-Xmas bonus. Four days later on Boxing Day, in the game with Livingston, it looked as if an additional two points were also in the process of being dropped. However, Larsson's injury time winner (after Jim Leishman's spirited side had twice equalised) meant a final score of 3-2 in favour of the leaders, ensuring a 100% home league record so far in the campaign. On the injury front, Chris Sutton, who was carried off during this engrossing contest, would now remain on the casualty list until early February.

As the year came to a close, those who follow the Celtic park club witnessed a return to Celtic's more ruthless side on December 29. The comprehensive 4-0 destruction of Dundee United at Tannadice (with goals from Hartson, Petrov, Thompson and Larsson) must have left the Taysiders somewhat green with envy. Celts would now greet 2002 not only ten points ahead of second place Rangers but also with the added luxury of a game in hand.

JANUARY 2002

Eric Black, in his new role as Motherwell manager, returned to the ground he knew well in early January but late strikes from both Larsson and Hartson (now a formidable partnership that boasted 33 goals) ensured a great start to another year by his former employer (2-0, 3.1.02). Lowly Alloa were then disposed of 5-0 in the Scottish Cup before an SPL trip down the west coast to face Kilmarnock at Rugby Park. Although Bobby Williamson's crew briefly troubled the reigning champions during the ninety minutes, goals from Hartson (again!) and Paul Lambert without reply sent those of a green persuasion back up the A77 in a relaxed frame of mind.

Although visitors St. Johnstone were still anchored firmly at the foot of the table, they certainly made a game of it on January 19 and actually opened the scoring. However, strikes from Larsson and Thompson were enough to settle the issue. All three goals, surprisingly, were netted in the first ten minutes of football! Hearts fared little better the following Wednesday as Larsson (with goal number 8 in 12 games against Craig Levein's side) and Moravcik did the damage that secured maximum points once more (2-0, 23.1.02). In defence of the Scottish Cup, a return visit to Kilmarnock in the space of just two weeks saw a repeat of the previous SPL scoreline although on this occasion defender Hay netted an own goal before Larsson struck in 62 minutes, welcoming a safe passage to Round 5 of the competition.

After an early setback at the Almondvale Stadium in West Lothian (Livingston drew first blood to lead at the interval), Celtic came good in the second period and netted three times in the month's final outing (3-1, 30.1.02). Moravcik (whose substitute appearance before the interval had helped turn the game), Larsson and Hartson were the scorers and the SPL trophy was just a little bit closer to being decked out in green and white ribbons for the second time in consecutive seasons. Reasons enough to be cheerful, to be sure.

As in the previous game with Livingston, Celtic were again behind at the break when they faced Franck Sauzee's Hibernian at Easter Road but a second-half header from John Hartson delivered a share of the spoils. Dreams of back-to-back trebles were ended when Rangers won a pulsating CIS Cup semi-final 2-1 at the national stadium but, with the championship still the obvious priority for Martin O'Neill's side, both Dunfermline and Dundee were made to suffer in pursuit of this main prize. First of all, the Fifers were humiliated 5-0 at Celtic Park (as Larsson claimed his first hat-trick of the season - despite missing a penalty!) before Dundee were drubbed 3-0 at Dens Park with both Hartson and Mjallby as well as Larsson doing all the damage.

The month's final fixture (a Scottish Cup Round 5 tie) took the 'Bhoys' back to the ground where they had lost in late December but this time the repeat 2-0 scoreline was in favour of Celtic and not Aberdeen. Although Henrik Larsson was missing, goals in either half from Hartson (who was later dismissed after a clash with Don Jamie McAllister) and Petrov meant a March Hampden semi-final clash with First Division outfit Ayr United. Once again, Chris Sutton was dominant at the heart of the Celtic rearguard.

With both Hartson (suspended) and Sutton (injured) not available for selection, Celtic faced Aberdeen again one week later minus a powerful, bustling centre-forward as partner to Henrik Larsson. That made little difference to the eventual outcome of this league encounter which was won with a Thompson penalty on the stroke of half-time and watched by over 59,500 supporters (1-0, 2.3.02). At a windy Ibrox eight days later, Stilian Petrov opened the scoring midway through the first forty-five, sliding the ball under the advancing Klos after a lovely pass from Larsson. Earlier, a good Hartson goal had been wrongly judged offside. Although Rangers equalised through defender Numan in the second-half to earn a share of the points, the championship was not within their reach.

The All-Ireland Hurling Championship trophy made an appearance at Celtic Park before kick-off with Dundee United the following week but the home fans were surely thinking of another piece of silverware. Mathematically, at the end of the ninety minutes, the title was now only two wins away after Stilian Petrov's goal (very similar to the one he claimed in Govan the previous week) kept his team's 100% home record intact (1-0,16.3.02). A short trip along the M8 three days later to face the amber shirts of Motherwell at Fir Park resulted in another extremely impressive showing by the 'Hoops' with Paul Lambert surely scoring one of the goals of the

season in just eight minutes. Another three in the second period without reply (two from Larsson and one from Johan Mjallby) highlighted the huge gulf between the teams and meant that, for Celtic, the SPL victory line was now only a trio of points away. Incidentally, midfielder Lambert would shortly be voted Scottish Football Writers' Player of the Year as well as being honoured in due course with the same award by club magazine, Celtic View.

Ayr United, in the Scottish Cup semi-final of March 23, proved to be as formidable as most SPL outfits and kept the game at 0-0 for the first forty-five minutes. However, after the interval, Celtic stepped up a gear and Larsson netted just four minutes after the restart. Two late Alan Thompson strikes completed the scoring. Away from the official football action, the club held a charity training session 'open day' in the east end of Glasgow later that week and drew a quite remarkable crowd of 11,000 fans to Celtic Park.

APRIL 2002

The first game of the month was the day that everybody had been waiting for – Championship Day! Obviously visitors Livingston, contenders for a UEFA Cup place, were not there just to make up the numbers but, after just three minutes, they fell

behind and their immediate footballing future was looking rather bleak indeed. So it proved as Larsson (scorer of that early goal) went on to claim his hat-trick with Hartson netting the other two in an astonishing 5-1 rout. Incidentally, the Swede and the Welshman had now hit a total of 56 goals between them. Martin O'Neill's Celtic had their second successive SPL title and the early season dream of two-in-a-row had become reality. Signed, sealed and delivered!

Despite the championship being out of harm's way, the team showed no sign of easing-up the following Saturday when Jimmy Calderwood's Dunfermline returned to the east end of Glasgow for the third time that season. In another classy show for the fans, Celts turned on the style yet again and blasted their second 'high five' in consecutive games despite the absence of top scorer Henrik Larsson. Goals from Paul Lambert, Jamie Smith and Momo Sylla joined John Hartson's double on the list of credits (5-0, 13.4.02). Hapless Dunfermline had now lost a total of 13 goals at Celtic Park in all league meetings this season.

The final home game of the campaign in late April was against Rangers and ended all square after first-half strikes from Lovenkrands and Alan Thompson confirmed a 1-1 draw. Although Celtic's 100% league record in the east end of Glasgow had now been breached, a total of 55 points from a possible 57 (and 51 goals scored with the loss of only 9) were really quite, quite remarkable statistics and something to be immensely proud of. Away to Hearts in the penultimate league game of 2001/02, the 'Bhoys' hit the 100 point mark for the season when Martin O'Neill's 'reserves' (with the Scottish Cup Final in mind, the manager made ten changes to the previous week's line-up against Rangers) crushed Craig Levein's Edinburgh side 4-1. Doubles from both teenager Simon Lynch (back to fitness after a pelvic injury had ruined his season) and Shaun Maloney (who also missed an injury-time penalty) plus a superb display by Jamie Smith kept the Celtic fans smiling.

MAY 2002

Disappointment followed on Scottish Cup Final Day (May 4) however when, despite being ahead twice during the game (with goals from Hartson and then Balde), Celtic eventually lost 3-2 to their oldest rivals. Four days later in Yorkshire, for Gary Kelly's charity benefit at Elland Road, some 7000 Celtic fans witnessed an impressive display of attacking football in the 4-1 victory over Leeds. Goals from Alan Thompson (a tremendous 35 yard left-foot drive), Henrik Larsson, John Hartson and Shaun Maloney kept the travelling support in party mood.

On Sunday May 12, Aberdeen was the last Scottish port of call for Season 2001/02. With several players either rested or injured, only Robert Douglas, Bobo Balde and Stilian Petrov remained from the previous week's defeated Scottish Cup Final team. The only goal of the game came from a superb Shaun Maloney free-kick twenty minutes before the end when the youngster found the top left-hand corner of the net from some thirty yards out. In truth, it was a strike good enough to win a championship let alone an end of season encounter with little at stake. With the final whistle came the realisation that Celtic had now amassed an astonishing 103 points for the campaign. Some total, some team! The following evening, the SPL trophy took its final bow for the season when Tom Boyd paraded the silverware at Highbury when English Champions Arsenal played the Scottish title holders in Tony Adams' testimonial game. Alan Thompson's first-half strike was cancelled out in the second period by Lee Dixon's headed goal to tie the match 1-1. With this friendly, Season 2001/02 was finally over.

In the league campaign, Celtic had played 38 games with a record of 33 wins, 4 draws and just 1 defeat. Martin O'Neill's side had also scored 94 goals with the loss of only 18. Quite simply, it had been another glorious season in the sun.

SEASON 2001/02 LEAGUE CHAMPIONSHIP QUIZ

1. Who opened the scoring for Celtic on the first day of the season?

2. Where did Henrik Larsson claim his opening goal of the campaign?

3. How many times did Celts score five at home?

4. Name the above opponents.

5. Which SPL outfit were the only team to score twice in one game at Celtic Park?

6. What was unusual about the Celtic team that lined up against Dunfermline on 8.9.01?

7. Neil Lennon's first goal of the campaign was scored against which side?

8. What was rather unusual about the 2-1 victory over St. Johnstone in January 2002?

9. Name the Celtic scorer when Rangers visited in April 2002.

10. John Hartson claimed his first hat-trick for the club against which of the Tayside clubs?

ANSWERS ON PAGE 62

ALMOST PERFECT

At a glance, Celtic's almost perfect home league record for Season 2001/02 when they scored 51 goals with the loss of only 9:

28.7.01 Celtic 3   St. Johnstone 0
Lambert (2), Mjallby

11.8.01 Celtic 2   Hearts 0
Larsson (2)

8.9.01 Celtic 3   Dunfermline 1
Moravcik (2), Sutton

22.9.01 Celtic 2   Aberdeen 0
Larsson, Petrov

20.10.01 Celtic 5   Dundee United 1
Hartson (3), Balde, Maloney

27.10.01 Celtic 1   Kilmarnock 0
Valgaeren

25.11.01 Celtic 2   Rangers 1
Valgaeren, Larsson

1.12.01 Celtic 3   Hibernian 0
Hartson (2), Lennon

15.12.01 Celtic 3   Dundee 1
Larsson, Sutton, Hartson

26.12.01 Celtic 3   Livingston 2
Larsson (2), Moravcik

2.1.02 Celtic 2   Motherwell 0
Larsson, Hartson

19.1.02 Celtic 2   St. Johnstone 1
Larsson, Thompson

23.1.02 Celtic 2   Hearts 0
Larsson (2)

9.2.02 Celtic 5   Dunfermline 0
Larsson (3), Hartson, Agathe

2.3.02 Celtic 1   Aberdeen 0
Thompson

16.3.02 Celtic 1   Dundee United 0
Petrov

6.4.02 Celtic 5   Livingston 1
Larsson (3), Hartson (2)

13.4.02 Celtic 5   Dunfermline 0
Hartson (2), Lambert, Smith, Sylla

21.4.02 Celtic 1   Rangers 1
Thompson

MISSING WORD QUIZ

Fill in the missing name (player or team) from Season 2001/02 Football Headlines. The clue is in the date!

'----- keeps out Celtic' Sunday Times, 19.8.01

'Celtic stumble but ---- take plunge' Daily Mail, 23.8.01

'Bhoys blow into town to flatten forlorn ----' Daily Mail, 27.8.01

'------- leaps in twice' Sunday Times, 16.9.01

'No case for ---- defence' Sunday Herald, 23.9.01

'------- wiped out by rub of the green' Daily Mail, 1.10.01

'Celtic strike ---- in time' Sunday Herald, 28.10.01

'Heavy Duty -------' Sunday Herald, 2.12.01

'Star ------ never looks out of place' Daily Mail, 17.12.01

'Heart-breaker ------- is the nemesis again' Daily Mail, 26.9.01

ANSWERS ON PAGE 62

TEAM CELTIC QUIZ

1) Who was the first player to score a double for Celts in Season 2001/02?

2) Celtic were already three goals up by half-time at Easter Road in late August 2001. True or false?

3) Who first appeared wearing the green in the game with Dunfermline in September 2001?

4) The same player scored his first Celtic goal against which team the following month?

5) How many doubles did John Hartson claim prior to his two strikes on Championship Day in April 2002?

6) Five players made a total of ten European appearances each in Season 2001/02. Can you name them?

7) Who opened the scoring against Rangers at Ibrox in both league encounters?

8) How many league goals did Celtic net at home during Season 2001/02?

9) Apart from Larsson and Sutton, who scored for Celts when Juventus were famously beaten 4-3 in the Champions League game of October 2001?

10) What was similar about the April 2002 home games with Livingston and Dunfermline?

ANSWERS ON PAGE 63

IF YOU KNOW THE HISTORY

CELTIC

THE HONOURS

SCOTTISH LEAGUE CHAMPIONSHIPS (38 IN TOTAL)

1892/93, 1893/94, 1895/96, 1897/98, 1904/05, 1905/06, 1906/07, 1907/08, 1908/09, 1909/10, 1913/14, 1914/15, 1915/16, 1916/17, 1918/19, 1921/22, 1925/26, 1935/36, 1937/38, 1953/54, 1965/66, 1966/67, 1967/68, 1968/69, 1969/70, 1970/71, 1971/72, 1972/73, 1973/74, 1976/77, 1978/79, 1980/81, 1981/82, 1985/86, 1987/88, 1997/98, 2000/01, 2001/02.

SCOTTISH CUPS (31)

1892, 1899, 1900, 1904, 1907, 1908, 1911, 1912, 1914, 1923, 1925, 1927, 1931, 1933, 1937, 1951, 1954, 1965, 1967, 1969, 1971, 1972, 1974, 1975, 1977, 1980, 1985, 1988, 1989, 1995, 2001.

SCOTTISH LEAGUE CUPS (12)

1956, 1957, 1965, 1966, 1967, 1968, 1969, 1974, 1982, 1997, 2000, 2001.

SPECIALS

European Champions' Cup 1967

Coronation Cup 1953

St. Mungo Cup 1951

Victory in Europe Cup 1945

Empire Exhibition Trophy 1938

Scottish League Commemorative Shield 1904/05 – 1909/10

Glasgow Exhibition Cup 1902

29

PICK OF THE TROPHY ROOMS

THE EMPIRE EXHIBITION TROPHY 1938

Thousands of visitors converged on Bellahouston Park in Glasgow for the Empire Exhibition of 1938 which had been formally opened by King George V1 and Queen Elizabeth on May 3. To commemorate the occasion, a tournament featuring clubs from both Scotland (Celtic, Rangers, Hearts and Aberdeen) and England (Chelsea, Sunderland, Brentford and Everton) was played at nearby Ibrox Park and attracted attendances to match. After all, it was not too often that world class players such as centre-forward Tommy Lawton and Joe Mercer (Everton) and Torry Gillick (Sunderland) were seen north of the border.

A crowd of some 54,000 saw Celtic's opening game with Sunderland which ended in a no score draw. The following evening, however, the 'Bhoys' netted three times (Divers 2 and Crum) in a 3-1 victory and progressed to meet Hearts in the next round. Johnny Crum scored again as the Edinburgh side were beaten 1-0 and Celts were through to the final where the mighty Everton, conquerors of both Rangers (2-0) and Aberdeen (3-2) would provide the opposition. Mighty Everton, indeed, as the English outfit had no fewer than ten internationalists (from all four home countries) at their disposal!

The final on June 10 was viewed by an 82,000 crowd who enjoyed a great game with little between two very fine sides. It was left to the marvellous Johnny Crum who, seven minutes into extra-time, netted his third goal in three games, ensuring that this unique trophy was bound for the east end of the city (on the back of a 1-0 score) and a permanent place of honour in the trophy rooms. Incidentally, to this day, Crum's jersey from the game (as well as the match ball) are also on display at Celtic Park.

Another Celtic legend, Jimmy Delaney, believed the team that lifted the Empire Exhibition Trophy was the best side he ever played with.

Celtic: Kennaway, Hogg, Morrison, Geatons, Lyon, Paterson, Delaney, MacDonald, Crum, Divers and Murphy.

John Thomson Memorial Cabinet.

IF YOU KNOW THE HISTORY

JOHN THOMSON
A CELTIC LEGEND

On 5 September 1931, defending champions Rangers met unbeaten Celtic at Ibrox in the league title race of Season 1931/32. Early in the second period, with the score standing at 0-0, 'Bhoys' brilliant young goalkeeper John Thomson dived bravely at the feet of Ranger Sammy English as the centre-forward shot from some ten yards. With his head covered in bandages, Thomson was carried from the field (suffering from a depressed fracture of the skull) and rushed to hospital but tragically died later that night at Glasgow's Victoria Infirmary. He was just twenty two years old.

After making his Celtic debut as a teenager against Dundee in February 1927, John Thomson went on to win Glasgow Cup medals in 1927, 1928 and 1930 as well as the Scottish Cup in 1927 and 1931. Naturally gifted with strong hands and wrists, agile as a cat and extremely courageous (he had previously suffered a fractured jaw saving against Airdrie in February 1930), the 'keeper was rightly considered to be the best of the best by those fortunate enough to have seen him in action.

His death affected not just football supporters throughout the land but also people in all walks of life. At the funeral, over twenty thousand people filled Queen Street Station and the surrounding streets of Glasgow as his coffin made its journey back to the small village of Cardenden in Fife where he was born. Celtic and Scotland had lost a very special son.

PICK OF THE TROPHY ROOMS

BENFICA EAGLE 1969

In Season 1969/70, Jock Stein led his team to their second European Cup Final after beating Leeds United both home and away at the 'semi' stage. The 'Eagle' (pictured here) is the club crest of twice European Champions Benfica who presented this stunning trophy to Celtic when the clubs met in the second round of that year's competition.

The 'Bhoys' really turned on the style in the first leg in Glasgow and scored three times although, in truth, their superiority warranted more. Such was Celtic's dominance that strikers Eusebio and Diamentino were replaced by defenders in order to keep the score down! First-half goals from Tommy Gemmell (in just two minutes) and Willie Wallace were complimented by a second period strike from Harry Hood thus ensuring a commanding 3-0 advantage for Portugal.

The return leg, however, presented an entirely different scenario and Celts lost two goals just before the interval. In a second-half that seemed to last an eternity, Benfica eventually claimed a third some two minutes into injury time to tie the game 3-3. As there was no more scoring in extra time, the outcome was decided (remember this was back in 1969) by the toss of a coin. Captain Billy McNeill guessed correctly!

Celtic: Fallon, Craig, Gemmell, Murdoch, McNeill, Clark, Johnstone, Hood, Wallace, Auld and Hughes. Brogan and Callaghan replaced Clark and Hood respectively for the return in Portugal.

MARTIN O'NEILL

Now in his third year with the club, Irishman Martin O'Neill guided his charges to a famous Scottish domestic treble of League, League Cup and Scottish Cup in his first season at Celtic Park. This was the first time in 32 years that a Celtic team had achieved this memorable feat. Although neither of the cups were delivered in period 2001/02, the SPL Championship Trophy (without question, the main event!) was retained by his team who amassed a quite astonishing points total of 103 for the season and won every home game bar one in the campaign.

ROBERT DOUGLAS

Firmly established as the team's number one goalkeeper, Robert Douglas arrived at the club in the winter of 2000 following his transfer from Dundee. Missed only four games in Season 2001/02 and headed the 'appearance' chart with a grand total of 51 outings in all competitions. Conceded just 17 goals and kept a clean sheet 28 times. Although one of those occasions was not the UEFA Cup game in Spain against Valencia (1-0 to the home side), his superlative performance that night was applauded not only by Santiago Canizares, one of Spain's best goalkeepers, but also by both locals and visitors alike that viewed the action. Earlier in the season, also on European duty, his saves in the Glasgow game with Ajax were just as important, helping his side through to the Champions' League Group Stage for the very first time. After Celts had drawn 1-1 with Rangers in March 2002 (and virtually secured the championship), Sky's 'Man of the Match' Lorenzo Amoruso suggested that Douglas should have been given the accolade following his series of superb second-half stops as the Ibrox side pushed for the winner.

JOOS VALGAEREN

Joos Valgaeren missed the latter part of Season 2001/02 (from early February to closedown in May) because of injury which resulted in two separate hernia operations. Prior to that, the Belgian central defender had been quite immense alongside Mjallby and Balde (and even Chris Sutton on occasion!) in a Celtic rearguard that conceded an average of less than one goal a game in a total of 32 outings. He even managed to hit the target himself in the SPL encounters with Kilmarnock (1-0, 27.10.01) and, most importantly, Rangers (2-1, 25.11.01) as well as Juventus in the never to be forgotten 4-3 Champions' League victory at Celtic Park in October 2001. Now in his third year with the club, Valgaeren never gives less than 100% effort for the cause.

JOHAN MJALLBY

Only one of two players (the other was Robert Douglas) who made more than a half century of appearances for Celtic last season, the Swede was one of Martin O'Neill's players of the year. Not surprising when you consider his rock-like performances at the heart of Celtic's back three week after week! The manager was quoted as saying 'He has been consistently there for us all the time. He plays the matches when he is not always completely right with fitness. He never wants to miss a game and his attitude is brilliant, as is his general play as a defender.' A true winner who is never ready to accept defeat, Mjallby scored the first league goal of the campaign in Season 2001/02 when St. Johnstone were beaten 3-0 at Celtic Park on late July's Flag Day. Additional strikes came in away games with both Dundee (3-0, 17.2.02) and Motherwell (4-0, 19.3.02) as the 'Bhoys' headed non-stop for the winning line. The defender actually began his Celtic career in central midfield when Dr. Jozef Venglos was in charge of the team. Of course, both Mjallby and fellow countryman Henrik Larsson spent the early part of Summer 2002 in the Far East on World Cup duty with Sweden. It came as no great surprise to see both players performing superbly in the company of the world's best.

BOBO BALDE

Dianbobo Balde made his debut in a Celtic jersey when Dunfermline visited (and lost 3-1) in September 2001 before claiming his first goal in the 5-1 demolition of Dundee United later the following month. By that time, with nine 'Hoop' appearances under his belt, this giant of a man had already made his way into the hearts of the Celtic faithful who had taken wholeheartedly to his strong, unyielding style of defensive play. Even at this early stage of his career in Scotland, his impact on the game is such that few opposition forwards relish the prospect of lining up against him. Balde started in thirty-eight games in period 2001/02 and scored two goals in each of the three Scottish domestic competitions. Surprisingly, the defender was the only Celt to score at Hampden on two separate occasions last season - in early February, he equalised against Rangers in the CIS Insurance Cup semi-final and then, three months later, gave his side a 2-1 lead early in the second-half of the Scottish Cup Final.

STEPHEN CRAINEY

The young left-sided defender appeared in Celtic's starting line-up a total of thirteen times last season and duly impressed on each occasion. At Ibrox in March (his first-ever Old Firm derby), Crainey was genuinely outstanding in the white heat atmosphere and seemed to stroll through the game as the 'Bhoys' took another giant step towards consecutive league championships. Some six weeks later, when Rangers visited the east end of the city (for the second 1-1 draw in a row), it was another performance of exceptional maturity by the former Celtic Boys' Club member. Not so long ago, there were genuine fears for his career as Stephen had developed glandular fever and, due to medical staff's concern about any possible infection, the twenty-one-year-old was actually banned from Celtic Park at one stage. Thankfully, he made a full recovery but not before wondering, throughout those long months of illness, if he would ever play football again.

DAVID FERNANDEZ

The 26-year-old Spaniard (first brought to the country by Airdrie boss Steve Archibald) joined Celtic on a four year contract in early summer 2002 after completing a memorable season with his second Scottish club, Livingston. Indeed, the West Lothian club had surprised most of the pundits by securing a very creditable third-place in the championship table despite only recently acquired SPL status. Fernandez, who had a spell with Deportivo La Coruna in Spain, was shortlisted for the SPFA Player of the Year award last season after a series of impressive performances for Jim Leishman's Almondvale side. A forward of tremendous natural ability, he had attracted the attention of a number of clubs before signing for the 'Bhoys' in a £1 million deal. There is no doubt that Fernandez will prove to be a great asset (both home & abroad) for Martin O'Neill's side.

DIDIER AGATHE

Scored the second of Celtic's three goals in the Amsterdam Arena when Ajax were put to the sword in early August 2001 (3-1, 8.8.01). That night, the Dutch just had no answer to his blistering pace and delightful skills. Until November last season (and the league game with Hearts at Tynecastle), Didier Agathe was virtually an ever-present in the starting line-up with a total of nineteen appearances in twenty-three matches. That winter's day in Edinburgh, however, he was badly injured in a tackle by the home side's Andy Webster (penalty, Larsson, 1-0 final score) and would subsequently be out of action until the following February when he again starred in his comeback game against Rangers at Hampden in the CIS Insurance Cup. Four days later, Agathe was one of the Celtic scorers when Dunfermline were blitzed 5-0 in the Glasgow league encounter. Most 'Hoop' fans still cannot believe that Martin O'Neill snapped up the player from Hibernian for a bargain fee of just £35,000 back in September 2000.

NEIL LENNON

Although the tenacious midfielder only managed one goal in Season 2001/02 (the 3-0 defeat of Hibernian at the beginning of December was the occasion), the Northern Ireland international turned in a series of tremendous performances for Celtic throughout the various Scottish and European campaigns. December 2000 was the date that Neil Lennon had arrived in Glasgow following his £6 million transfer from Leicester City where he had been Martin O'Neill's trusted on-field lieutenant. In the first Old Firm derby of last season (2-0, 30.9.01), Lennon was quite magnificent in a 'Man of the Match' display that completely stifled the creativity of Ronald de Boer. When Rangers were beaten 2-1 in the league championship game of late September, it was Lennon's pass that led to the (converted) Larsson penalty and all three points as Celtic raced 10 points clear of their great rivals in the title race. In last season's final clash with the Ibrox side (May's Hampden Scottish Cup date), it was simply a case of a game too far for the player who was due go under the knife and have immediate surgery to rectify knee problems that started after the 3-2 Boxing Day joust with Livingston and had been endured ever since. Who can say what the outcome might have been that day at the National Stadium if Neil Lennon had been 100% fit?

STILIAN PETROV

The young Bulgarian's first outing for Celtic last season was when Dunfermline were beaten 3-1 in early September. The following week, Petrov scored in the City of Discovery after appearing as a substitute (for Lubo Moravcik) in the 4-0 rout of Ivano Bonetti's Dundee at Dens Park. Then, striking a rich vein of goalscoring form, it was a case of three goals in just four games against both Scottish and European opponents – Juventus (2-3, 18.9.01), Aberdeen (2-0, 22.9.01) and Rangers (2-0, 30.9.01). The midfielder's rather important opener in the aforementioned SPL encounter with Rangers at Ibrox (a wicked free-kick that completely deceived 'keeper Klos) broke the deadlock early in the first-half, setting the 'Bhoys' on the road to an essential victory. Incidentally, this was Celtic's third Old Firm clean sheet in a row. Stilian Petrov (SPFA Young Player of the Year for Season 2000/01) repeated his feat of three goals in four games towards the latter part of last season when championship glory was waiting just over the horizon. The matches in question this time featured Aberdeen in the quarter-final of the Scottish Cup (2-0, 25.2.02) in addition to both Rangers (1-1, 10.3.02) and Dundee United (1-0, 16.3.02) in the league.

ALAN THOMPSON

Quite rightly, many fans of Celtic considered Alan Thompson's goal against Old Firm rivals Rangers at Ibrox to be one of the season's most memorable. Cast your mind back to the end of September 2001 and the league encounter in Govan when the 'Bhoys' were leading 1-0, deep into injury time. Ghosting past members of the blue rearguard, the Englishman cut in from the left-hand side of the park before releasing a delightfully angled right-foot shot which curled past 'keeper Klos to the instant acclaim of those several thousand supporters directly behind the German's bulging net. A true peach of a goal! It should not be forgotten that, the previous season, it was the same player whose name was on the goal that sunk Rangers 1-0 in the crucial February league encounter. Considered by many to be the complete midfielder, the player was also responsible for netting the winner in the games with Rosenborg (1-0, 10.10.01), St. Johnstone (2-1, 19.1.02) and Aberdeen (1-0, 2.3.02). In total, 'Geordie Lad' Thompson claimed nine goals last season, making him the club's third top scorer behind strikers Larsson and Hartson - if you do not include Shaun Maloney's four goals in the CIS Insurance Cup match with third division Stirling Albion.

HENRIK LARSSON

Even to those folk who are not Celtic-minded, it came as no great surprise to see the name of Henrik Larsson (surely the complete striker?) at the top of the SPL scoring chart for Season 2001/02. His final tally of 35 goals (in 47 games) was 10 ahead of his closest rival, Tore Andre Flo of Rangers. Although the electric Swede did not score in the opening league encounter of the campaign (when visitors St. Johnstone travelled from Perth for the day), he claimed the winner the following week when Celts defeated Kilmarnock 1-0 at Rugby Park in early August. In fact, the forward netted the deciding goal in a total of ten European and domestic games last term with hat-tricks being achieved twice. On Championship Day last April (one of those hat-trick occasions), it was surely fitting that Larsson scored both the first and last Celtic goals of the afternoon. With barely two minutes on the clock, he hit a low shot past Livingston 'keeper Broto following Paul Lambert's cut-back. Then, early in the second period, Lambert was again the provider for an easy Swedish finish. Under Martin O'Neill, the striker had hit the back of the net an astonishing 88 times, with his Celtic career to date not far short of that magical 100. In the World Cup finals of summer 2002, Larsson netted three times for his country (making it a grand total of 24 goals in 72 international games) as they progressed to the last sixteen of the tournament. However, following Sweden's exit at the hands of shock troops Senegal, Henrik announced his retirement from international football.

CHRIS SUTTON

Chelsea fans were always full of praise for Chris Sutton's impeccable centre-half performances when he wore their colours some years ago. In last season's SPL game with Hearts in Glasgow (2-0, 11.8.01), he turned in a commanding man of the match performance when asked to fill the same defensive position (for the very first time) in the green of Celtic. Unfortunately, Sutton missed quite a few games because of injury last term but, when available for selection, he was always never less than impressive regardless of his function in the team. As a striker, he claimed his first of the season in the Champions League qualifier with Ajax of Holland in the Amsterdam Arena. Celtic's third of the night, it was a superb second-half header from Didier Agathe's perfectly inviting cross. In total, the Englishman played 29 games throughout the season and claimed seven goals in the process, including doubles in the encounters with Hibernian at Easter Road (4-1, 25.8.01) and Juventus in the classic 4-3 Champions League joust of late October. The latter game was, of course, one of those special European nights which will never be forgotten by anyone with Celtic in their heart.

SHAUN MALONEY

When Celtic met Stirling Albion in Round 3 of the CIS Insurance Cup competition in early November 2001, Shaun Maloney hit four goals in the 8-0 rout, becoming the only Celt to reach this total in any one game last season. In all, the young striker netted ten times in domestic competition including an impressive double against Hearts at Gorgie Road in late April's SPL encounter. His first goal that afternoon in the capital was a magnificent free-kick curled into the far corner of Niemi's net which even brought applause from the master, Lubo Moravcik, on the substitutes' bench. Yes, it was that good! The youngster also claimed Celtic's last goal of Season 2001/02 when another stunning free-kick from some thirty yards left Ryan Esson (in the Aberdeen goal) without a prayer.

JOHN HARTSON

Following his £6.5 million move from Coventry last early August, Welshman John Hartson arrived in Glasgow with Season 2001/02 just one game old. He then made his 'Hoops' debut (albeit as substitute) a couple of days later when Celtic travelled to Ayrshire for the SPL match with Kilmarnock. Although the fans had to wait somewhat longer to acclaim his first goal for the club (October to be precise), the occasion, when it arrived, was really quite special – a hat-trick in the 5-1 demolition of Dundee United! By season's end, Hartson had netted 24 times in 35 games including doubles in the clashes with Stirling Albion in the CIS Insurance Cup (8-0, 6.11.01) and Hibernian (3-0, 1.12.01), Dunfermline (4-0, 9.12.01), Livingston (5-1, 6.4.02) and Dunfermline again (3-0, 13.4.02), all in the league title race. On the wonderfully emotional day that the championship was officially retained, he scored with a sweet, low volley in nineteen minutes and then, six minutes later, a powerful header gave 'keeper Broto no chance as Celts stormed to a 3-0 advantage early-on in the game. His last goal of that period (and, indeed, his first Old Firm strike) was at Hampden in the Scottish Cup Final when another header gave his side the lead in the penultimate game of the season.

TO BE THE BEST
PAUL LAMBERT

It came as no great surprise to the Celtic faithful when, at season's end, club captain Paul Lambert was confirmed as the Football Writers 2001/02 Player of the Year in Scotland. Indeed, in their eyes, it had been a foregone conclusion for some considerable time since, right from the start of league business, the player had simply been immense. Throughout the season, week in and week out, his form rarely dipped, leading by example as the 'Bhoys' secured the Scottish Premier Championship for the second year running.

To the surprise of many neutral observers, when St. Johnstone were Flag Day visitors on a day trip to Glasgow in late July, it was Lambert (Man of the Match) who claimed two of Celtic's three goals in this opening domestic encounter. He would net a total of five during the season with the other three coming, after the turn of the year, in the games with Kilmarnock (2-0, 12.1.02), Motherwell (4-0. 19.3.02) and Dunfermline (3-0, 13.4.02).

Lambert's ninth minute strike in the Fir Park encounter with Motherwell (when Celts already had their fingers on the SPL silverware) was certainly a 'Goal of the Season' candidate. Collecting the ball some forty yards out, he worked one-twos with both Hartson and Larsson before beating 'keeper Dubourdeau from close range. As well as being a peach of a goal, it also settled the nerves on a night when three points meant that the team could now retain the league trophy by winning their next game - which just happened to be taking place at Celtic Park!

Paul Lambert's name was included in last season's starting line 48 times, a figure only surpassed by 'keeper Robert Douglas and defender Johan Mjallby who both totalled 51 appearances. For the second year in a row, the midfield partnership of Lambert and Neil Lennon was an unqualified success although it was most unfortunate that neither of them were fully fit for the Hampden date with Rangers in early May. If that had been the case, the outcome of the Scottish Cup Final may have been quite different.

All footballers hope to scale the heights in their relatively short careers. There is no doubt that Paul Lambert (European Cup winner with Borussia Dortmund) reached the top of his profession some considerable time ago. And the simple fact remains - he's still there!

CELTIC TRUE?
CELTIC FALSE?

1) Dundee are the only team to have won at Celtic Park in Season 2000/01 or Season 2001/02. **True or false?**

2) John Hartson scored 22 goals in Season 2001/02. **True or false?**

3) Celtic won the championship by defeating Rangers 3-2 in the last 'Hoops' league game of Season 1978/79. **True or false?**

4) The Scottish Cup was lifted eight times during Jock Stein's time as manager of the club. **True or false?**

5) Excluding the strikers, Alan Thompson was Celtic's top scorer last season. **True or false?**

6) The sports newspaper 'France Football' named Celtic as 'European Team of the Year' in Season 1966/67. **True or false?**

7) Celtic won the first-ever 'Old Firm' encounter (28th May 1888) by a margin of 4 goals to 2. **True or false?**

8) Henrik Larsson scored a total of 52 goals in all competitions during Season 2000/01. **True or false?**

9) 'Dixie' Deans claimed a hat-trick in the 6-1 Scottish Cup Final win over Hibs in 1972. **True or false?**

10) Ex-manager Wim Jansen played for Feyenoord when the Dutch side met Celtic in the 1970 European Cup Final. **True or false?**

CELTIC TRUE?
CELTIC FALSE?

ANSWERS ON PAGE 63

TWO-IN-A-ROW QUIZ

1) How many times have Celtic now won the Scottish League Championship?

2) Who were Celtic's opponents on Championship Day, 7th April 2001?

3) Henrik Larsson claimed 34 goals in Season 2001/02. True or false?

4) Name the 'Bhoy' who scored a double when Rangers were defeated 3-0 at Ibrox in late April 2001.

5) Although no longer at the club, this player netted twice on his debut when Aberdeen came calling in December 2000. Who was he?

6) Where did the 'Hoops' drop their first points of Season 2001/02?

7) The September 2001 victory over Rangers was the first back-to-back Ibrox victory in how many years?

8) Robert Douglas only missed two league games before the 2001/02 Title was secured. Name the opposing teams.

9) He scored goal number 5 in just 3 SPL games when Dundee were beaten 3-1 in mid-December 2001. Was it Larsson, Sutton or Hartson?

10) Who did Celtic defeat 4-0 in the league game before Championship Day 2002?

ANSWERS ON PAGE 63

CELTIC IN EUROPE QUIZ

- Name the scorers when Leeds United were beaten 2-1 at Hampden in the 1970 European Cup semi-final.

- What was unusual about the outcome of the Celtic/Benfica second round European Cup tie of Season 1969/70?

- Celtic defeated Rosenborg 5-2 on aggregate in the 1972/73 European Cup. What happened to the Norwegian goalkeeper Karlsen afterwards?

- When Celtic won the European Cup in 1967, it was the first time that this trophy had been won by a team of home nationals. True or false?

- How many times had Celtic's opponents that day, Inter Milan, previously lifted the famous trophy?

- Who scored the only goal when Rosenborg lost 1-0 in Glasgow, October 2001?

- Whose European goal scoring record did Henrik Larsson break in the December 2001 game with Valencia?

- Celts reached the semi-final of the European Cup Winners' Cup in Season 1963/64. True or false?

- The 1970 European Cup Final was played at which famous stadium?

- Name the Lisbon Lions.

ANSWERS ON PAGE 63

58

Quiz Answers

HEADLINE NEWS

1) Paul Lambert scores twice in the opening game of the season
2) Celts beat Ajax 3-1 in the Amsterdam Arena
3) Reference to 4-0 victory at Dens Park   4) 3-2 defeat by Juventus in Italy
5) 4-3 victory over Juventus   6) A new SPL record of 10 consecutive league wins
7) Celts beat Rangers 2-1
8) Celts win 3-1 in Dundee but the Dens Park floodlights go out for 15 minutes
9) Celts 4-0 victory over Dundee United
10) Ex-Celt Tommy Johnson's late equaliser for Kilmarnock against Rangers

SEASON 2001/02 LEAGUE CHAMPIONSHIP

1) Johan Mjallby. 2) Rugby Park, Kilmarnock. 3) Four times.

4) Dundee United, Dunfermline (twice) and Livingston. 5) Livingston.

6) The starting line-up did not include a single Scot. 7) Hibernian, 1.12.01.

8) All three goals were scored in the first ten minutes. 9) Alan Thompson.

10) Dundee United.

MISSING WORD QUIZ

1) Broto (ref. Livingston 'keeper's performance in the 0-0 draw)
2) Ajax (ref. their 1-0 win in Glasgow)   3) Hibs (ref. 4-1 Easter Road victory)
4) Larsson (ref. striker's goals in 4-0 win over Dundee)
5) Dons (ref. Celtic's 2-0 triumph)   6) Rangers (ref. 2-0 Old Firm victory)
7) Joos (ref. Valgaeren's winner in the 1-0 Kilmarnock game)
8) Hartson (ref. striker's two goals in 3-0 win over Hibernian)
9) Sutton (ref. his midfield performance in the 3-1 Dundee triumph)
10) Larsson (ref. his goal in the 1-0 win over Porto in the Champions League)

TEAM CELTIC QUIZ

1) Paul Lambert in the opening game of the season
2) False – it was 4-0 at half-time! 3) Bobo Balde 4) Dundee United
5) Four, if you include his hat-trick against Dundee United in October 2001
6) Johan Mjallby, Rab Douglas, Paul Lambert, Henrik Larsson and Neil lennon
7) Stilian Petrov 8) 51 goals 9) Joos Valgaeren
10) Celts scored five times on each occasion.

CELTIC TRUE? CELTIC FALSE?

1) True 2) False – it was 24 3) True 4) True 5) True – with 9 goals
6) False – it was in Season 1969/70 7) False – it was 5-2 8) False – it was 53.
9) True 10) True.

TWO-IN-A-ROW QUIZ

1) 38 times 2) St. Mirren 3) False – it was 35 goals 4) Lubo Moravcik
5) Ramon Vega 6) Livingston 7) 17 years 8) Dunfermline and Kilmarnock.
9) John Hartson 10) Motherwell

CELTS IN EUROPE QUIZ

1) John Hughes and Bobby Murdoch
2) After a 3-3 aggregate score, Celtic progressed on the toss of a coin
3) He signed for Celtic 4) True 5) Twice 6) Alan Thompson
7) Jimmy Johnstone 8) True 9) San Siro in Milan
10) Simpson, Craig, Gemmell, Murdoch, McNeill, Clark, Johnstone,
Wallace, Chalmers, Auld and Lennox

CELTIC

SCOTTISH PREMIER LEAGUE CHAMPIONS

SEASON 2001/02

	P	W	D	L	F	A	PTS
CELTIC	38	33	4	1	94	18	103
RANGERS	38	25	10	3	82	27	85
LIVINGSTON	38	16	10	12	50	47	58
ABERDEEN	38	16	7	15	51	49	55
HEARTS	38	14	6	18	52	57	48
DUNFERMLINE	38	12	9	17	41	64	45
KILMARNOCK	38	13	10	15	44	54	49
DUNDEE UTD	38	12	10	16	38	59	46
DUNDEE	38	12	8	18	41	55	44
HIBERNIAN	38	10	11	17	51	56	41
MOTHERWELL	38	11	7	20	49	69	40
ST. JOHNSTONE	38	5	6	27	24	62	21